THE NATURE KIDS GUIDE TO THE
DUCK BILLED PLATYPUS

DAVID ANDERSON

LP Media Inc. Publishing
Text copyright © 2026 by LP Media Inc.
All rights reserved.

For information address LP Media Inc. Publishing,
30012 Variolite St NW, Princeton MN 55371
www.lpmedia.org

Publication Data

Duck Billed Platypus
The Nature Kid's Guide to Duck Billed Platypuses — First edition.

Summary: "Learn all about the Duck Billed Platypus, the Nature Kid Way"
— Provided by publisher.

ISBN: 979-8-89818-133-8

[1. Duck Billed Platypus – Non-Fiction] I. Title.

Title: The Nature Kid's Guide to Duck Billed Platypuses

CONTENTS

RIVER HOMES

Splash! A platypus dives into a cool stream. It disappears underwater.

Duck-billed platypuses live in rivers and streams. They make their homes in eastern Australia. The water there is clean and cool.

Platypuses dig **burrows** in riverbanks. The entrance is often hidden underwater. This keeps the platypus safe inside.

They like rivers with rocky bottoms. Rocks and logs give them places to rest. Trees along the banks give shade and shelter.

Platypuses can spend up to 17 hours each day in their burrows. They block the tunnel with dirt. This keeps them hidden, warm, and dry.

AUSSIE ONLY

Squish! A platypus walks on a muddy bank. It is in Australia.

Platypuses live in one place on Earth. They live in Australia. No other place has them! This makes them very special.

You can find them on the east coast. They live from Queensland to Tasmania.

Some live near warm rainforests in the north. Others live high up in the cold Australian Alps. A small group even lives on Kangaroo Island. People brought them there long ago.

Platypuses have lived in Australia for over 100 million years. That is older than dinosaurs!

POCKET
SIZED

Peek! A young platypus follows its mother out of it's burrow.

Platypuses are small animals. They are about the size of a house cat. Most weigh only 2 to 5 pounds.

Males are bigger than females. A male can be 20 inches long. Females are usually around 17 inches.

Their flat tails add even more length. A tail can be 5 inches long. This tail also stores fat for energy.

Baby platypuses are called Puggles and are born without fur and with closed eyes.

BIZARRE BODIES

Whoosh! A platypus swims by. Its flat body glides smoothly.

Platypuses have very strange bodies. They look like a mix of different animals! Scientists were confused when they first saw one.

They have a bill like a duck. But it is soft and rubbery, not hard. Their webbed feet help them swim.

Thick, waterproof fur covers their body. This special fur keeps them warm and dry underwater.

Platypuses have no teeth as adults. Instead, they use rough pads in their mouths to crush their food.

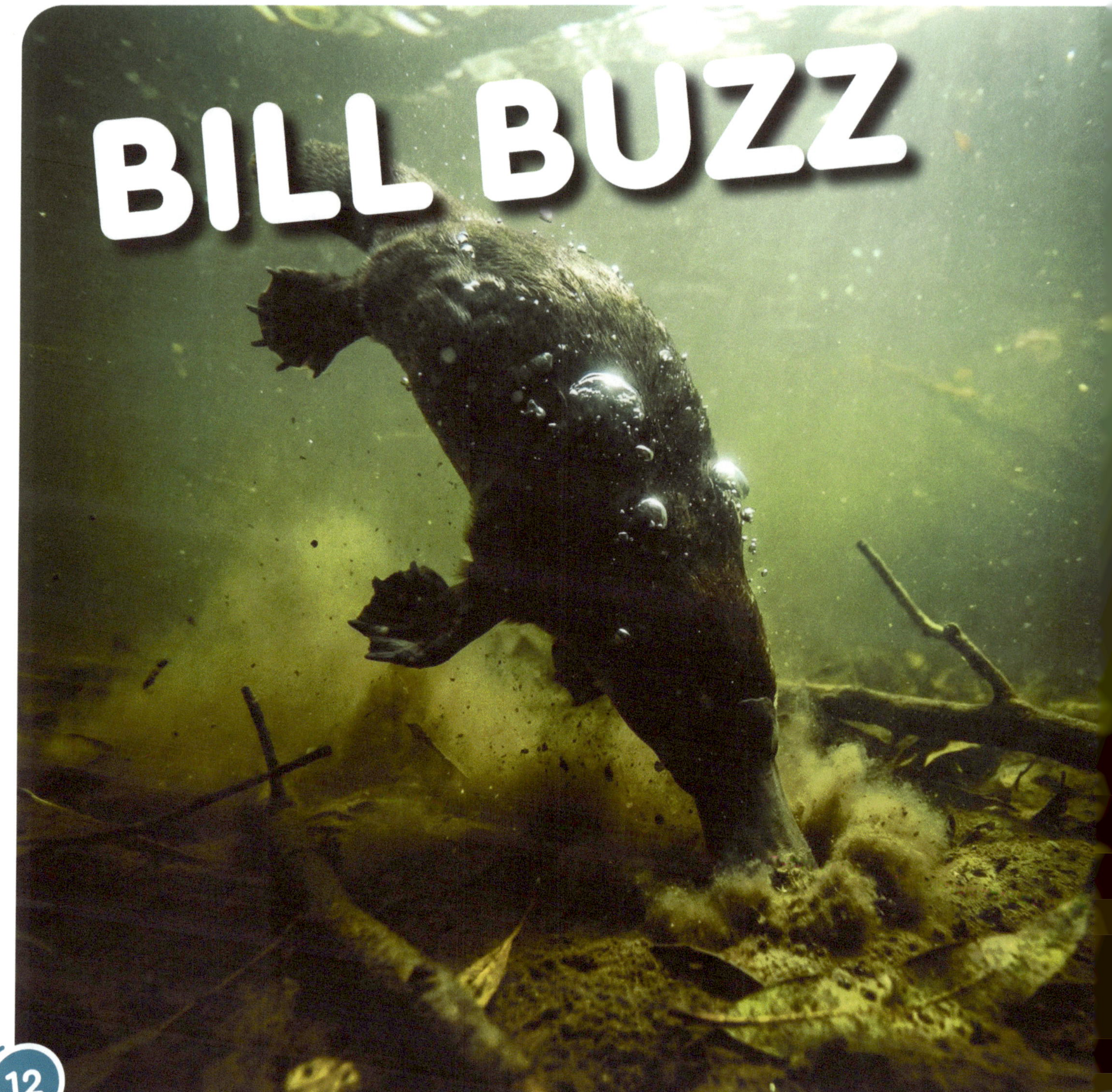
BILL BUZZ

Swish! A platypus moves its bill side to side in the water.

A platypus bill is amazing. It can sense things we cannot! The bill feels tiny electric signals.

All living things make electricity. Muscles make small electric pulses. The platypus feels these signals with its bill.

The bill also feels touch. It senses movement too. This helps it find food in dark, muddy water.

A platypus bill has about 40,000 electric sensors in its skin.

VENOMOUS
KICK

Thump! A male platypus kicks with its back leg. Sharp spurs stick out.

Male platypuses have sharp spurs on their back ankles. These spurs can deliver **venom**!

Only males have working spurs. Females are born with them too, but they fall off.

The venom is strong enough to kill dogs. It is very painful to humans. The pain can last for weeks!

This makes the platypus one of few venomous mammals on Earth.

Males make more venom during mating season. Scientists study it for new medicines.

YUMMY
YABBIES
16

Crunch! A platypus chews food on the riverbed.

Platypuses eat many small creatures. They love yabbies. Yabbies are freshwater crayfish from Australia.

They also eat shrimp. They eat insect larvae too. Worms and small fish are yummy treats.

A platypus has special cheek pouches. It stores food in them. It can collect food underwater. Then it floats up to eat.

Platypuses eat a lot each day. They eat about 20 percent of their body weight.

Platypuses can eat up to 1,000 worms in one night!

DIVE DEEP
FUN FACT!
A platypus can dive up to 30 feet deep to search for food on the river bottom.

Swoosh! A platypus dips below the surface. Its eyes close tight.

Platypuses hunt underwater with their eyes shut. They close their eyes, ears, and nose when they dive. They rely only on their special bill to find food.

A platypus can stay underwater for about two minutes. It dives down to the bottom of rivers and streams, where it digs through mud and gravel.

The platypus uses its bill to scoop up prey, sweeping back and forth along the riverbed.

Platypuses hunt for several hours each night. They make hundreds of dives to catch enough food.

WATCH OUT

DID YOU KNOW?
Goannas are large lizards. They raid platypus burrows to eat eggs.

Rustle! Something moves in the reeds. The platypus must stay alert.

Platypuses have many **predators**. Large water rats hunt young platypuses. Foxes and wild dogs catch them on land.

Birds are dangerous too. Wedge-tailed eagles have sharp eyes. They spot platypuses swimming below.

In some northern rivers, saltwater crocodiles are a big threat. These huge reptiles can catch a swimming platypus.

Young platypuses are most at risk. They are small. This makes them easy targets.

BURROW BOUND

Scratch! A platypus digs into the soft, muddy riverbank.

Platypuses hide in burrows. This keeps them safe. These tunnels are dug into riverbanks. The door is often under the water.

A resting burrow can be up to 30 feet long. The tunnel twists and turns in the dirt.

Inside, the platypus is safe. The narrow tunnel keeps out big animals.

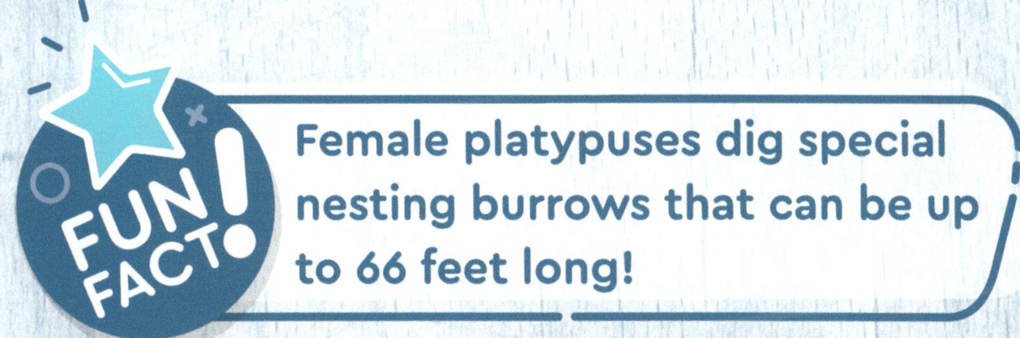

SWIM STARS

Glide! A platypus zooms through the water. Its webbed feet push hard.

Platypuses are excellent swimmers. They can swim up to 2 miles per hour!

Their front feet have large webs that work like paddles. They use their back feet and flat tail to steer.

On land, platypuses walk slowly. Their front webs fold back under their feet like closed umbrellas. This stops the webs from tearing on the ground.

Platypuses row with their front legs. Most swimming mammals use their back legs instead!

26

Snap! A platypus pops up from the dark water. Evening has come.

Platypuses are **nocturnal**. This means they are most active at night.

During the day, platypuses rest in their burrows. They sleep curled up in a cozy nest.

At dusk, they come out to hunt. They spend about 10 to 12 hours searching for food in the dark water.

Their special bill helps them find prey without seeing it. Darkness is no problem for a platypus!

When platypuses sleep, their bills twitch and move side to side. Scientists think they might be dreaming about hunting!

SOLO
SWIMMERS
28

Quiet! A platypus swims alone, with no friends nearby.

Platypuses live alone. They do not form groups or families.

Each platypus has its own home range. A male's range can stretch up to 9 miles along a river.

Males and females only meet to mate. Then they go their separate ways.

A platypus is happy to hunt and sleep by itself.

Platypuses recognize each other by smell. Each one has a unique scent from skin glands.

WATER
WALTZ

Chirp! A female platypus swims by the river. A male follows her.

Platypuses mate once a year. Their mating season is from June to October.

The male swims after the female. He may hold her tail with his bill.

After mating, the male leaves. He does not help raise the babies.

The female digs a nesting burrow. She blocks it with dirt plugs so no one else can get in. This keeps her safe inside.

Male platypuses swim in circles around females. This water dance is part of courtship.

MUDDY EGGS

Platypus eggs have a sticky shell. When the mother lays them, the eggs stick together and stick to her belly.

Shhh! A tiny pink puggle is growing its egg. Its skin has no fur yet.

Platypuses are one of only five mammals that lay eggs. A mother lays one to three small eggs.

The eggs are soft and leathery, about the size of marbles. The mother keeps them warm for about ten days.

When puggles hatch, they are very tiny. Each one is about the size of a bean! Their eyes are not open yet.

Puggles stay in the burrow for three to four months. They grow fur and learn to swim before leaving.

MAMA MILK

A mother platypus curls around her puggles in the dark burrow.

Platypus mothers make milk for their babies. But they do not have nipples like other mammals.

The milk oozes out through patches of skin on the mother's belly. Puggles lick the milk right off her fur.

Mother's milk is very rich, which helps puggles grow fast and stay healthy.

Puggles drink milk for about four months. After that, they are ready to find their own food.

Platypus milk fights germs. Scientists study it to make new medicines!

36

Wow! The platypus is one of Earth's strangest animals.

The platypus looks like no other animal on the planet. It has a bill like a duck. It has a tail like a beaver. It has feet like an otter!

It is one of only two mammals that lay eggs. The echidna is the other one.

Scientists call them **monotremes**. This name means egg-laying mammals. No other group is like them in the entire world.

When scientists first saw a platypus long ago. They thought it was fake! They looked for stitches holding the parts together.

PROTECT PLATYPUS

Rumble! Trucks dig near the river. Platypus homes are in danger.

Platypuses need clean rivers to live. Trash and dirty water can hurt them. It is hard to find food in dirty water. Over time they have lost about 40% of their original habitat.

People help by keeping rivers clean. Picking up litter helps platypus homes stay safe.

Some rivers have safe zones. These areas help platypuses find food. They can raise their babies there too.

Platypuses are near threatened. This means they need human help to keep their habitats safe.

GLOSSARY

burrows
Tunnels that animals dig underground to live in.

venom
A poison that some animals make in their bodies.

nocturnal
An animal that sleeps during the day and is awake at night.

predators
Animals that hunt and eat other animals.

monotremes
Special mammals that lay eggs instead of having live babies.